E. B. WHITE ROOM

STO LAT

The Spirit of POLAND

by Roger Jan Radlowski
and John J. Kirvan

Winston Press

Library of Congress Catalog Card Number: 79-55964
ISBN: 0-03-056666-7

Translated into Polish by Robert C. Geryk, Maria T. Geryk,
and the Rev. Henry Andrzejczak. Papal text translated
into Polish from the official English version.

Art Direction and Photo Editing: Keith McCormick and Miriam Frost
Design: Ned Skubic

Printed in the United States of America.

5   4   3   2   1

Winston Press, Inc.
430 Oak Grove
Minneapolis, Minnesota 55403

The text of this book is set in ITC Zapf Chancery Light
and printed on 80 pound Productolith Dull by Viking Press, Inc.

Photography Credits

Craig/FPG: 25
Cullinen/FPG: 38–39
Dibble/Alpha: 19 (upper left and lower left)
Raymond Gawlak: 11, 12, 15, 19 (right), 22, 23,
    26–27, 40, 42, 43, 44, 45, 46, 47, 49, 50–51,
    56, 59, 60
Meyer/White Eyes Design: 10, 21
Nowak/Alpha: 18
P.A. Interpress: 1, 2, 14, 16–17, 20, 24, 30, 32,
    34, 35, 36, 37, 52
Allan A. Philiba: 13
Pix/FPG: 55
Rhoda Sidney: 8, 9
Vzoff/FPG: 28
Williamson/FPG: 29, 31, 33
Wolfe: Front and back cover

Locations of Special Interest

2: Members of a Kaszubian song-and-dance group,
    Kaszuby
13: Near Krakow
15: Near Limanova
17: Krakow's Cloth Halls—the thirteenth-century
    stalls, rebuilt in 1555 in the Renaissance style
18: Old town square, Warsaw
19 (lower left): Zakopane
19 (right): Szczecin
20: Member of a song-and-dance group, Rzeszow
21: Gdansk
23: Near Wadowice
25: Jasna Gora shrine, Czestochowa
26–27: Near Nowy Sacz
29: Cathedral and Copernicus Museum, Frombork
30: Wawel cathedral, Krakow
32: Children caroling, Jablonka
33: View from northeast side of Kasprowy Wierzch
35: A lacemaker of Koniskow
49: Near Olsztyn
50–51: Near Rabka
52: Pope John Paul II at the grave of his parents,
    Rakowicki Cemetery in Krakow
55: Church in Czchow
56: Near Olsztyn
59: Tatra Mountains

Wigilia Blessing

I wish you health.
I wish you wealth
that passes not with time.
I wish you long years.

Blessing

May your heart be as patient
as the earth
Your love as warm as harvest gold.
May your days be full,
as the city is full
Your nights as joyful as dancers.
May your arms be as welcoming
as home.
May your faith be as enduring
as God's love
Your spirit as valiant as your heritage.
May your hand be as sure as a friend
Your dreams as hopeful as a child.
May your soul be as brave
as your people
And may you be blessed.

From Pope John Paul II

"Praise be to Jesus Christ.
  Dear brothers and sisters,
  I would like to invite you to join me
  in professing our faith, our hope, and
  our fidelity to Mary, the Mother of
  Christ and of the Church, and also to
  begin again on the road of history and
  of the Church.

"Without Christ it is impossible to
  understand the history of Poland, the
  history of the people who have passed
  or are passing through this land. . . . I
  who am a son of the land of Poland
  and who am also Pope John Paul II, I
  cry from all the depths of this
  millennium, I cry. . . . Let your Spirit
  descend."

Błogosławieństwo wigilijne

Życzę Wam zdrowia.
Życzę Wam bogactwa, które nie przemija
z czasem.
Życzę Wam długich lat życia.

Błogosławieństwo

Niechaj serce Wasze będzie tak cierpliwe
jak serce ziemi
Wasza miłość tak ciepła jak żniwo.
Niechaj dni Wasze będą tak pełne jak
pełne jest miasto
Wasze noce tak radosne jak noce w tańcu.
Niechaj Wasze ramiona będą tak witające
jak progi domu.

Niech wiara Wasza będzie tak wytrwała
jak Boża miłość
i duch Wasz tak dzielny jak Wasze
dziedzictwo.
I ręce Wasze niech będą tak pewne jak
przyjaciel
i sny Wasze tak pełne nadziei jak dziecko.
Niech dusza Wasza będzie tak dzielna jak
Wasz naród.

Od Ojca Świętego, Jana Pawła II

Niech będzie pochwalony Jezus Chrystus!
Ukochani bracia i siostry,
Chciałbym Was zaprosić abyście
przyłączyli się do mnie we wspólnym
wyznaniu naszej wiary, naszej nadziei,
i naszej wierności ku Maryi, Matce
Chrystusa i Matce Kościoła, i we
wspólnej, od nowa, wędrówce szlakiem
historii i szlakiem Kościoła.

Bez Chrystusa niesposób zrozumieć
historii Polski, historii narodu, który
szedł i idzie przez tę ziemię... ...Ja,
który jestem synem polskiej ziemi i
który jestem papieżem Janem Pawłem
II—wołam z głębi milenium,
wołam... ...Przyjdź o Duchu Święty.

I wish you health.
I wish you wealth
that passes not with time.

I wish you long years.

May your heart be as patient
as the earth . . .

Your love as warm
as harvest gold.

May your days be full,
as the city is full . . .

$\mathcal{Y}$our nights as joyful as dancers.

*M*ay your arms be as welcoming as home.

*M*ay your faith be as enduring as God's love . . .

*Y*our spirit as valiant as your heritage.

*M*ay your hand be as sure as a friend . . .

Your dreams as hopeful as a child.

May your soul be as brave as your people...

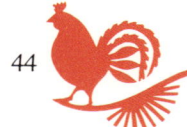

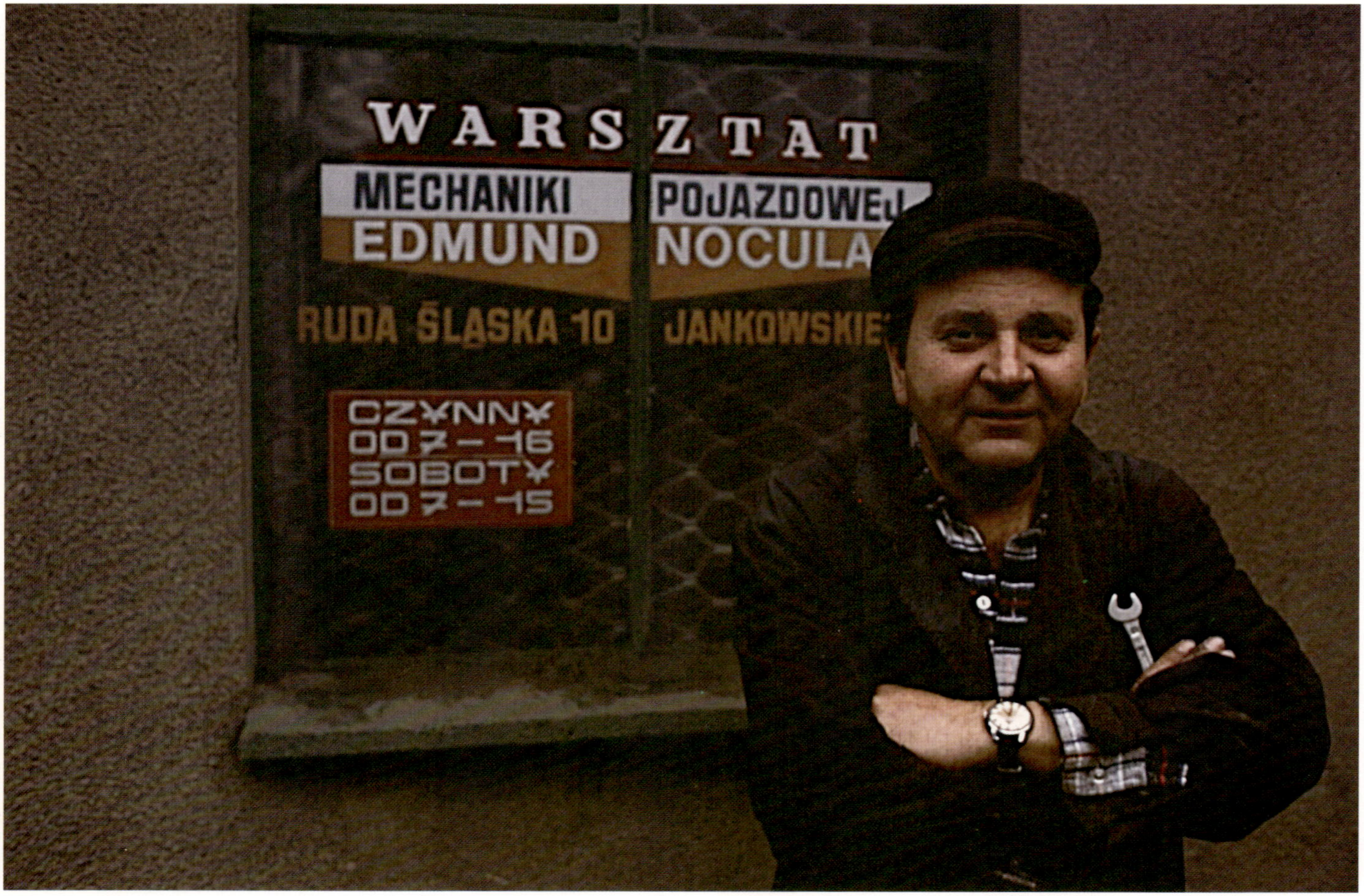
WARSZTAT
MECHANIKI POJAZDOWEJ
EDMUND NOCULA
RUDA ŚLĄSKA 10 JANKOWSKIE
CZYNNY
OD 7 – 16
SOBOTY
OD 7 – 15

And may you be blessed.

"Praise be to Jesus Christ.

Dear brothers and sisters,
I would like to invite you to join me
in professing our faith, our hope, and
our fidelity to Mary, the Mother of
Christ and of the Church, and also to
begin again on the road of history and
of the Church."

"*Without Christ it is impossible to understand the history of Poland, the history of the people who have passed or are passing through this land.... I who am a son of the land of Poland and who am also Pope John Paul II, I cry from all the depths of this millennium, I cry.... Let your Spirit descend.*"

"*Let your Spirit descend
and renew your life
as it renews the face of the earth . . .*

"The face of this land."